Motorbooks International

MIL-TECH SERIES

M1 ABRAMS
MAIN BATTLE TANK

The Combat and Development History of the General Dynamics M1 and M1A1 Tanks

Michael Green

To my good friend Sfc. James L. Edwards (US Army) who got me started in the writing business

First published in 1992 by Motorbooks International Publishers & Wholesalers, PO Box 2, 729 Prospect Avenue, Osceola, WI 54020 USA

© Michael Green, 1992

Motorbooks International is a certified trademark, registered with the United States Patent Office

The information in this book is true and complete to the best of our knowledge. All recommendations are made without any guarantee on the part of the author or Publisher, who also disclaim any liability incurred in connection with the use of this data or specific details

We recognize that some words, model names and designations, for example, mentioned herein are the property of the trademark holder. We use them for identification purposes only. This is not an official publication

Motorbooks International books are also available at discounts in bulk quantity for industrial or sales-promotional use. For details write to Special Sales Manager at the Publisher's address

Library of Congress Cataloging-in-Publication Data
Green, Michael.
 M1 Abrams main battle tank / Michael Green.
  p. cm.
  Includes index.
  ISBN 0-87938-597-9
  1. M1 (Tank) I. Title.
  UG446.5.G69 1992
  358.1'883—dc20   91-48212

On the front cover: An M1 Abrams in the California desert at the National Training Center, Fort Irwin. *Greg Stewart*

On the back cover: Top, a 3rd Infantry Division M1 in West Germany. *US Army* Below, a three-view drawing of the M1 tank. *General Dynamics*

Printed and bound in the United States of America

Contents

Acknowledgments

Special thanks for help in putting this book together go to Dick Hunnicutt, Greg Stewart, Laurie Viggiano, Donald L. Gilleland, Bill Rosenmund, Col. David Kiernan, Nat Dell, Pedro Marrero, Maj. John Bernhard, *Armor Magazine* and AFV News.

Armor Might

The tank is the most important ground-assault weapon with the greatest battlefield survivability of all US combat vehicles. The tank provides the US military with mobility, shock effect, lethality and the mounted combat capability essential for conducting a war of movement—as demonstrated during Operation Desert Storm.

During the large tank battles of the Persian Gulf War, M1A1 tanks suffered very few losses while hundreds of Iraqi tanks were destroyed by US tank units. Stories of astonishing performances by M1A1 tankers abound. For instance, Company B of the United States Marine Corps' 4th Tank Battalion (a reserve unit), in their M1A1s, took on an Iraqi brigade during a night engagement on 24 February 1991. The result was a 119:0 kill ratio. This occurred only twenty days after Company B completed New Equipment Training on the M1A1, where they operated the tank for the first time. The US Army's 24th Infantry Division (Mechanized), spearheaded by nearly 300 M1A1s, covered over 200 miles of the most rugged desert terrain of southern Iraq in less than thirty-six hours.

Reliability, mobility, survivability and combat effectiveness of the Abrams tank were all successfully demonstrated in Operation Desert Storm. US Army acquisition chief Steven Conver told members of US Congress immediately after the Middle Eastern conflict that the M1A1s "were impervious to T-72 and T-55 tank rounds" during battles with Iraq. The Abrams' performance, crew protection and firepower are elements that set this system apart from all other main battle tanks. The confidence of the tanker was conclusively demonstrated on the Middle Eastern battlefield. In reference to the tank battles that were then taking place, General Schwarzkopf stated at his press conference that "I would tell you that one of the things that has prevailed, particularly in this battle out here, is our technology." This M1 system, which emerged from a solid US technological and industrial base, will continue to maintain that technological edge—providing its crew with maximum combat effectiveness on tomorrow's battlefield.

*Armor might indeed! A line of M1 Abrams
tanks prepare to fire their guns on the range
at Fort Bragg.* General Dynamics

Chapter 1

A Brief History

During the Middle Ages, Leonardo da Vinci and other inventors designed vehicles for war that were horse-powered, bristling with guns and could carry a crew. Unfortunately, horses tend to get very tired very quickly. Some thought

The most well known American tank of World War II was the M4 Sherman. Almost 18,000 various models of the M4 were built during the war. The six basic models of the M4 Sherman tank differed in various ways, ranging from engines to hull construction. In general, they weighed in at about thirty tons, were protected by one to three inches of armor and had a crew of five. US Army

The final version of the M4 Sherman tank also saw service during the Korean War. Here, American and South Korean soldiers *are being protected by an M4A3 (76mm gun) Sherman tank.* US Army

Early prototype of the M48 tank undergoing mobility testing at Aberdeen Proving *Ground, Maryland, on 12 April 1952.* US Army

An M48A1 tank fitted with a roller-type mine exploder that has just set off a large antitank mine during tests conducted by the US Army in late 1957. US Army

Known as the T-67 flame-thrower tank, this vehicle was based on the M48A1. Pictured in use by the Marine Corps in March 1961 at Quantico, Virginia, during a firepower display. On the right is an Ontos antitank vehicle. Used by the Corps during the Vietnam War, this vehicle was equipped with six 106mm recoil-less rifles. USMC

was also given to providing such vehicles with sails, but the undependable nature of the wind soon discouraged thought in that direction.

It wasn't until the nineteenth and twentieth centuries that self-propelled vehicles became possible. In 1801 the caterpillar track was invented, and

The M48A3 tank saw widespread use by the US Army during the Vietnam War. This vehicle belonging to the 11th Armored Cavalry Regiment sports the nickname the Wild One 4. *US Army*

steam-powered engines for moving artillery were experimented with through the middle 1800s.

When German engineer and inventor Gottlieb Daimler displayed the internal-combustion engine in 1886, military forces in every part of the world set to work to apply this new and powerful source of power to warfare. Machine-gun and light-cannon carriers were evolved through the early 1900s. But, much like the ancient horse-drawn chariots, a disadvantage was encountered. The carriers were heavy and restricted to the best roads; cross-country movement was virtually impossible.

The beginning of the M60 series of tanks began with a modified M48A2C fitted with a 105mm gun and new front hull. Shown is an early-model M60 tank at Aberdeen Proving Ground, Maryland, on 21 March 1961. Early-model M60 tanks had the same type of rounded turret as the M48 tank. US Army

It was the type of stalemate produced in France during World War I by the machine-gun and trench warfare in 1914 that spurred on military minds to develop an armored vehicle capable of traveling over battlefield terrain and over enemy trenches. England introduced the first tank in warfare on the battlefields of France on 15 September 1916. The new machine proved effective in silencing machine-gun emplacements and demoralizing enemy troops.

The years between 1918 and 1939 saw considerable improvement in tanks and the birth of modern tank tactics. The armored division came into being and was used considerably in World War II. Depending on the country, armored divisions could possess from 100 to 300 tanks and 8,000 to 15,000 soldiers. In the US Army, Gen. George Patton demonstrated the tremendous potential of this highly mobile and hard-hitting force.

As the M4 Sherman tank was the symbol of American armor units during World War II, the M48 tank and its successor, the M60, became the mainstay of American armor might during the postwar years.

Entering service with the US Army in 1953, almost 12,000 various models of the M48 were manufactured between

The M60 tank was soon provided with a new, elongated (or needle-nose) turret that provided superior armor protection. This M60A1 tank of the US Marine Corps was photographed on 9 December 1976. USMC

1953 and 1959. The early models were beset with technical problems ranging from the difficult fire control system to poor overall mechanical reliability. As with any complex piece of new machinery, there are usually teething problems. All new tank designs, be it American, Soviet, German and so on, have to go through this cycle before all the bugs can be worked out. Eventually the defects in early-model M48 tanks were corrected, leading to the fielding of the M48A5 Patton tank in US military service.

No longer in service with the American military, the M48A5 last saw action with the United States Army National Guard. In its final form in American service, the M48 tank became essentially an M60. It was equipped with the same gun, fire control system, engine and so on as the M60, mounted in the M48 Patton tank hull and turret. The upgraded M48 tank was a useful and cost-effective way to upgrade the American Army's tank fleet during the 1970s when a shortfall of M60 tanks left the

The last version of the M60 series of tanks was the M60A3. The main difference between this model and earlier versions was an upgraded fire control system. Michael Green

American armor forces sadly lacking in numbers against the massive Soviet tank fleets based in Eastern Europe.

M60 Tank

The story of the M60 tank began in 1959 when a modified version of the M48 Patton tank was produced with a new hull, a diesel engine and a 105mm gun. It was redesignated as the 105mm gun tank M60. The M60 series of tanks had always been considered to be only an interim vehicle intended to serve the US Army until the ideal tank could be designed and built. But, over 15,000 tanks later, the M60 is still in service with the US Army. Numerous improvements helped to extend the service life of the tank.

With the ending of American military involvement in the Vietnam War, the US Army found itself in the unbearable position of lagging behind the Soviet Union in armor technology. While the M48A3 Patton tank had served its purpose well in Vietnam, it was not the equal of then currently fielded Soviet-built tanks like the T-62.

Soviet T-62 main battle tank, armed with a high-velocity smoothbore 115mm antitank gun. The T-62 first entered production in late 1961. Over the years it has been supplied to many countries, yet, in combat it has fared poorly against Western-designed tanks. Michael Green

An Army MBT-70 prototype at Aberdeen Proving Ground, Maryland. US Army

The XM803 tank was basically a stripped down version of the MBT70, which it closely resembles. US Army

The M60 and M60A1 tanks first fielded in the early 1960s by the US Army were adequate, but, due to its relatively low rate of production, there was not going to be enough of them to help stem a Soviet military onslaught on Western Europe and the North Atlantic Treaty Organization (NATO) armies. The reason for this tragic state of affairs was that the United States became more and more involved in the Vietnam War, its attention and re-

sources were diverted from armor modernization. Unlike previous military conflicts such as World War II where technological advancements of weapon systems, like tanks, jumped by leaps and bounds, the Vietnam War resulted in a complete slowdown in technological development of American armor.

As soon as funding became available, the US Army embarked on a modernization of its tank fleet, including the upgrading of its M48 and M60 series

The first M1 pilot tank model. This vehicle carried the designation XM1; X stands for experimental. The X is dropped when the vehicle goes into full-scale production. US Army

There were eleven pilot-model XM1 tanks built for testing purposes. This XM1 is being loaded into the front of a US Air Force C-5 transport plane. Because of the weight of the tank, only one tank at a time can be carried. US Army

The first production model M1 tank, nicknamed Thunderbolt, *came off the production line in February 1980.* US Army

tanks. Unfortunately, these older generation vehicles, while equal to or better in some ways than many Soviet designed and built main battle tanks, would never be able to overcome the large imbalance in numbers between the American and Soviet tank fleets.

MBT-70

In 1967 a joint American-West German program began to create a prototype vehicle known as the main battle tank 1970 (MBT-70, for short). The MBT-70 had a three-person crew, all located in its turret. Using a hydro-pneumatic suspension system, the vehicle's height and clearance could be changed while moving to increase mobility and reduce vulnerability.

The MBT-70's main armament was a 152mm dual-purpose tube that could fire both antitank missiles or conventional tank rounds. Additional armament included a 20mm cannon for either ground or air targets, a 7.62mm coaxial machine gun and a grenade launcher for close-in protection. An automatic loader allowed rapid firing and accounted for the three-person crew on the vehicle.

Unfortunately, rising costs and technical problems resulted in the US Congress ending the program in 1970.

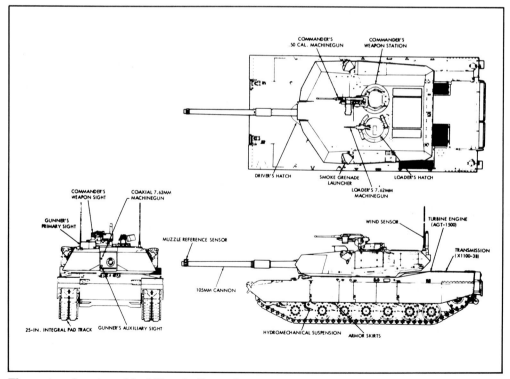

Three-view drawing of the M1 tank. General Dynamics

XM803

After the ending of the MBT-70 program, the US Army decided to try going ahead with a simpler version of the MBT-70 known as the XM803 tank. The vehicle was going to use only American made components to reduce cost and improve reliability.

The powerful turbine engine on the M1 tank, coupled with an advanced suspension system, allows the vehicle to practically fly across terrain that would bog down any other tank. The Abrams has incorporated many features including the turbine engine to avoid being detected, leading many European units to coin the phrase "whispering death" when referring to the Abram's ability to move quickly and quietly, and serves as a premier cavalry platform based on its success in numerous Reforger exercises. There is no higher compliment than to have the soldier in the field quickly adopt and gain confidence in a piece of equipment. US Army

Only one prototype of the MX803 tank was built. But the cost of the tank remained a problem. As a result, the US Congress canceled the XM803 tank program in 1971 and told the US Army to try to find a less costly tank to build.

XM1

A few months after the XM803 tank program was killed by the US Congress, the Army began looking for another future tank that could be designed and built under a very strict cost ceiling. The Army did not want to repeat the errors of the past two tank programs. As a result, in February 1972, the Army established at Fort Knox, Kentucky, the Main Battle Tank Task Force. This think tank of soldiers, civilians and developers was assigned the job of defining

M1 tanks of the 2nd Armored Division wait in a staging area during Reforger 1987 (West Germany).

the characteristics of what the Army wanted in a new tank and what the Army could afford.

Two companies, Chrysler Corporation and General Motors Corporation, involved in the task force came up with over a hundred different proposed tank designs to be considered and reviewed by the task force members.

In August of that same year, the Main Battle Tank Task Force finished its work by coming up with a report listing nineteen important characteristics they felt a future Army tank would

M1 tank in a defensive position at the National Training Center, Fort Irwin, California, 1985. Michael Green

*The first production models of the M1 tank
were fitted with a British-designed 105mm
gun.* US Army

need to survive and win on some future battlefield.

After being reviewed, the task force report eventually became a Development Concept Paper that was approved in early 1973 by the deputy secretary of defense.

In June of 1973, two companies, Chrysler and General Motors, were given contracts by the Army to produce a number of prototype vehicles that would possess the characteristics rec-

ommended by the Main Battle Tank Task Force.

Chrysler, besides making cars, had been building tanks for the US Army since World War II. General Motors had been the main contractor on both the MBT-70 and XM803 tank programs and were slightly reluctant to enter the competition for building the Army's new tank of the future.

Of the big three American auto makers, Ford Motor Corporation, which

Besides the 105mm main gun, the M1 tank is also armed with a 7.62mm machine gun fitted alongside the main gun and another on a flexible mount fitted to the loader hatch. The M1 tank commander position is provided with a .50 caliber machine gun. US Army

The M1 tank is an important part of the Army's combined arms team, which also in-cludes mechanized infantry and helicopters. US Army

An M1 tank at speed in West Germany, 1984. Michael Green

had built thousands of tanks for the US Army during World War II, had been interested in the new tank competition but was forced to drop out when the Department of Defense wouldn't let them use Israeli tank designers on their staff.

In October 1973, the Arab-Israeli Yom Kippur War broke out. In nineteen days of fierce fighting, some of the largest tank battles since World War II had been fought. Over 1,694 tanks had been destroyed or lost—roughly 420 Israeli and 1,274 Arab tanks.

Many of the Israeli Army tanks destroyed had been American-built M48 and M60 tanks. Using information from the Yom Kippur War on the performance

The M1 tank was first seen in Western Europe in late 1982. The first unit to receive the new tank was the 3rd Infantry Division. US Army

of both American and Soviet built tanks in battle caused a rethinking of some of the characteristics the Army was looking for in its future tank.

As a result, a new Tank Special Study Group was set up by the Army to suggest design changes to both Chrysler and General Motors in the building of their prototype vehicles.

The new tank under development was given the title of XM1. The X stands for experimental in the Army nomenclature system.

In early 1976, both Chrysler and General Motors presented their prototype vehicles to the Army for testing, the purpose of which was to decide which contractor provided the best tank at the lowest price. Both contractors' vehicles looked similar in overall design and were about equal in performance.

Also entered into the competition for the Army's new battle tank was a modified version of the West German Army Leopard II tank. After much controversy, the Department of Defense

Some of the first M1 tanks issued to US Army units in West Germany. These vehicles have just returned from the live-fire range. You can see the empty shell cases stacked in the vehicle side storage racks. US Army

announced at a news conference on 12 November 1976 that Chrysler had won a contract to build eleven pre-production pilot models of the XM1 tank for testing by the US Army.

The first pre-production pilot XM1 tank was delivered by Chrysler to the Army in 1978. On 7 May 1979, the Secretary of Defense approved low-rate initial production of 110 XM1 tanks by Chrysler. The vehicle was classified as

standard in February 1981 as the M1 Abrams.

In 1982, Chrysler Corporation sold its tank building division to General Dynamics. The new division became known as General Dynamics Land Systems. General Dynamics is best known for building F-16 fighter planes for the US Air Force and submarines for the US Navy.

Soldiers of the 3rd Infantry Division based in West Germany, taking part in a large-scale *tactical field exercise with their M1 tanks.* US Army

Due to the weight of the M1 tank, the normal means of transport is by Department of Defense railroad flat cars that were specially built to carry two M1 tanks at a time. Michael Green

In 1983, a few M1 tanks from the 2nd Armored Division were sent to Saudi Arabia for a demonstration tour for the Saudi army. *The Saudi military was most impressed with the vehicle's mobility and firepower.* FMC

The infantry counterpart of the M1 tank is the M2 Bradley Infantry Fighting Vehicle. The two vehicles are designed to work together on the battlefield. US Army

In an effort to reduce fuel consumption and engine wear, the Army proposed that an auxiliary power unit (APU) be mounted on the Abrams. The APU consisted of a 5.6 kilowatt diesel-powered generator, seen here mounted on the right rear of this M1 tank. The unit has not gone into production yet. US Army

Chapter 2

Vehicle Description

The first production model M1 tank rolled off the factory floor in February 1980. It was also given the name Abrams in honor of the late Gen.

Creighton Abrams, former chief of staff, US Army. General Abrams saw action during World War II as a lieutenant colonel in charge of the Fourth Division's

The commander of the M1 tank (left) is joined by the loader (right) who mans the 7.62mm machine gun, if needed. US Army

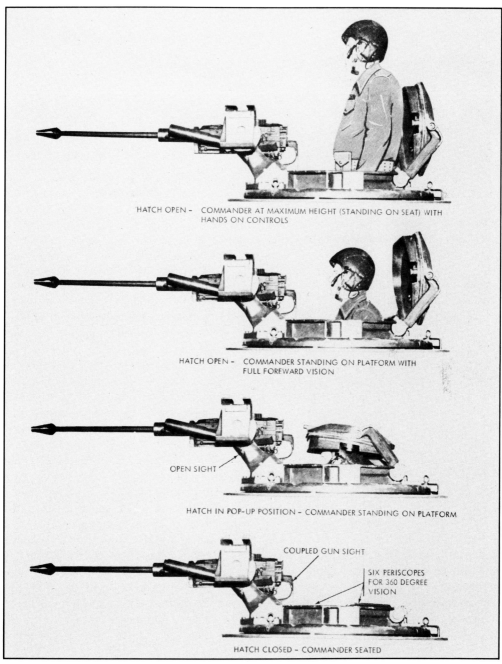

HATCH OPEN – COMMANDER AT MAXIMUM HEIGHT (STANDING ON SEAT) WITH HANDS ON CONTROLS

HATCH OPEN – COMMANDER STANDING ON PLATFORM WITH FULL FOREWARD VISION

OPEN SIGHT

HATCH IN POP-UP POSITION – COMMANDER STANDING ON PLATFORM

COUPLED GUN SIGHT

SIX PERISCOPES FOR 360 DEGREE VISION

HATCH CLOSED – COMMANDER SEATED

Various positions of the M1 tank command-er's hatch cover are illustrated. Chrysler

The .50 caliber machine gun position of the M1 tank commander. The .50 caliber machine gun is designed to be used against infantry and soft targets like trucks. But it can still penetrate lightly armored enemy vehicles if need be. US Army

37th Tank Battalion. He also commanded US forces in Vietnam as a four-star general.

The first production models of the basic M1 tank issues into regular Army use in 1981 weighed in at about sixty tons combat loaded. They were then armed with the same M68E1 105mm rifled main gun used on the M60 tank. Aside from its main gun, the first model M1 tanks were also equipped with a coaxial M240 7.62mm machine gun; a similar weapon on a flexible mount was fitted to the loader's hatch, and an M2HB .50 caliber machine gun was fitted to the tank commander's position.

The M1 Abrams was a revolutionary development for the Army's tank fleet. Equipped with normal steel armor and then state-of-the-art composite special armor which consisted of layers of both steel and nonsteel armor, the M1 tank was tested against almost all types of antitank rockets and missiles that had taken such a heavy toll on American-built Israeli Army tanks during the 1973 Yom Kippur War.

Another novel feature of the M1 Abrams was its Textron Lycoming AGT-1500 turbine engine. Far more reliable, smaller, quieter and less smoke-producing than diesel tank engines then in use with the Army, the powerful turbine engine on the M1 tank, coupled with an improved torsion bar suspension system, could push the M1 tank to speeds up to 45 mph (limited by an engine governor) on paved, level roads. Cross-country travel could be done at over 30 mph. In contrast, the M60 tank could barely make 30 mph on paved, level terrain and 15 mph cross country.

Additional advanced features fitted to the M1 tank were a fire control system featuring a laser range finder, ballistic computer, gunner's thermal-imaging day and night sight, fully stabilized turret, a muzzle reference sensor to measure gun-tube distortion and a wind sensor.

These advanced features allowed the M1's gun to be fired with great accuracy to the limit of its effective range, day or night, with a very accurate fire-on-the-move capability. Troop trials

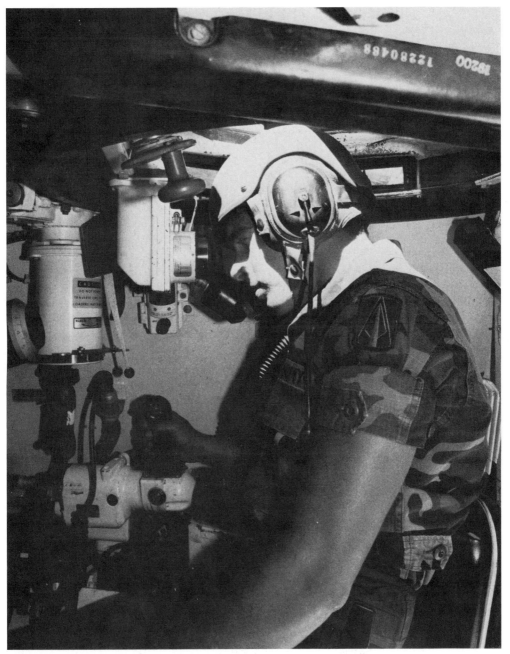

M1 tank commander's position. He is looking through the gunner's primary sight extension. Michael Green

conducted by the tankers of the First Cavalry Division, based at Fort Hood, Texas, in late 1980 showed that M1 tank crews could consistently achieve first-round hits at ranges in excess of one and a half miles while traveling cross country at 25 mph.

Tank Layout

The M1 tank's layout (or how the engine, transmission, gun and crew are placed in the tank) is an example of form following function. A tank's layout is driven by the tank's operation on the battlefield. The tank must move across country at comparatively high speed, carry powerful armament and protect its crew.

A tank hull is normally divided into three compartments: the driver's compartment, the turret area and the engine compartment. The engine of a tank is normally compartmentalized to reduce the chance of a fuel fire spreading into the crew areas. The engine is normally found in the front or rear of the tank. Although most tanks produced since World War II have the engine and transmission in the rear, many tanks produced before and during the war had the engine in the rear and the transmission in the front.

The M1 tank consists of the hull and turret. The turret can rotate a full 360 degrees. All electrical system connections between the hull and turret are made through a slip-ring mechanism.

In both the M1 and M1A1 tank, the driver is seated at the front of the hull center. The vehicle's commander and gunner are seated on the right of the turret, with the loader on the left side of the turret.

A power pack is located in the rear of the hull and provides basic power to drive the tank. The power pack includes a turbine engine mated to an automatic transmission. Accessories on the power pack provide hydraulic and electrical power for the tank and its auxiliary systems.

The multifuel turbine engine burns diesel or kerosene-based fuel mixed

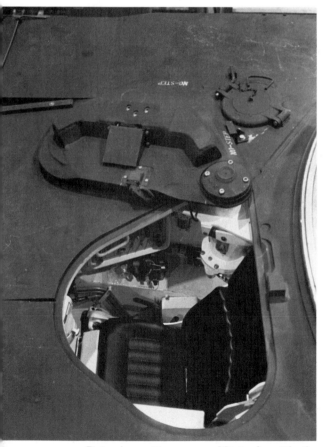

Driver's position on an M1 tank, with the driver's hatch in the open position. Michael Green

with compressed and heated air. However, it can burn a variety of hydrocarbon fuels including gas, alcohol and diesel, and all grades of jet fuel. The engine drives the transmission through a reduction gearbox.

The gas turbine engine uses a high-efficiency air cleaner and a series of connecting ducts, and air filtration systems to effectively ensure ninety-nine-percent clean air to the engine. In the late 1970s, early prototype test vehicles had a defective air-cleaner seal which allowed dust to contaminate the engine. Problems such as this are a fact of life during developmental and operational tests. Many news reports described this incident as a faulty engine design. In fact, it was an air filtration problem, which the US Army and the contractor quickly recognized and fixed. The seal was redesigned and there has never been another incidence of engine failure from design related dust ingestion. In extreme desert conditions, where the sand is very fine—like talcum powder—soldiers clean the air filters as a part of routine crew maintenance procedures. The Abrams has proven in its series of Middle East performance demonstrations and in combat during Operation Desert Storm, that, with adherence to proper maintenance procedures, the tank performs as flawlessly in the desert environments as anywhere else.

Driver Controls

The driver sits semireclined, and has three, hatch-mounted periscopes that provide excellent visibility exceeding 120 degrees.

Steering is accomplished by turning a motorcycle-type T-bar which actuates the steering lever on the transmission to produce the steering speed bias of the tracks. There is a twist grip control on the outside (right) of the T-bar that serves as the throttle for the electronic fuel management system and eliminates the need for a floor accelerator pedal, thus providing more foot space. Conditions of fluid levels, filters, batteries, electrical connectors and circuit breakers are displayed on the driver's instrument panel (DIP).

The transmission shift selector and push buttons for the intercom system

The M1 tank driver sits in a semireclined seat. US Army

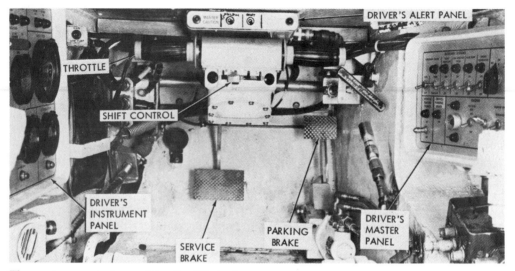

The various controls used by the M1 tank driver. US Army

The M1 tank's suspension system consists of fourteen road wheel stations (seven per side) with steel torsion bars at all positions. The
tank *also has two return rollers at the top of the hull, as shown. This tank is without its normal side skirt armor.* US Army

also are located on the T-bar assembly in the center. The service brake pedal is in the center of the floor, allowing braking with either foot. The driver's seat is adjustable for driving with the hatch either open or closed, and the seat height can be set to four different positions. A large knob on an adjustable lower lumbar support allows the driver to control the amount of lower back support. In combat the M1 tank driver's job is to constantly search for routes and firing positions which provide maximum protection from enemy fire. The driver also maintains a stable platform for firing on the move.

Suspension System

Although the capability to deliver accurate fire on the move is largely dependent on the efficiency of the gun and sight stabilization system, the tank's suspension system also plays a significant part. The suspension is designed not only to provide a gun platform that is as stable as possible, but to also minimize mine damage. It consists of fourteen road-wheel stations (seven per side) with steel torsion bars at all positions and advanced rotary shock absorbers installed internally.

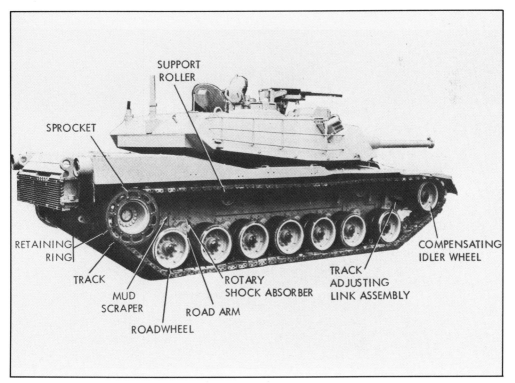

Details of the M1 tank suspension system.
General Dynamics

The four forward road-wheel stations are reinforced to form a box-like structure to resist mine damage. Aluminum tubes also seal these first bars from exposure to foreign matter from the bilges, and a transverse armored cover over the torsion bars provides the driver with added protection from mine blasts.

Turbine Engine

The 1,500 hp, multifuel, gas turbine engine provides significant advantages that offset its higher fuel consumption compared to conventional diesel engines. Most of the advantages make the Abrams tank safer in combat—and who would trade crew safety for a few gallons of fuel?

The turbine engine, which was originally selected for its superior reliability, was 2,000 pounds lighter than a comparable diesel. This weight difference was used to increase the tank's armor protection. The turbine has thirty percent fewer parts than the diesel, which makes it more dependable and easier to maintain. Unlike a diesel, the turbine engine will start at minus twenty-five degrees Fahrenheit, is very quiet (track noises are louder than the engine) and has practically no smoke signature. It requires

Overhead view of the AGT-1500 gas turbine engine at the factory, before being installed in the M1 tank. US Army

more filtered air for combustion than a comparable diesel, but less total air since the turbine does not require radiators, air passages and fans for cooling the engine.

Fuel accounts for less than one percent of the operational costs of the tank, and the performance advantages of a 1,500 hp gas turbine engine contribute greatly to crew survivability—which is the first consideration. Because a tank's fuel needs are an important part of logistic planning, the Abrams has a cruising

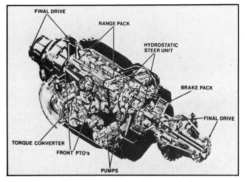

Cutaway drawing of the M1 tank transmission. General Dynamics

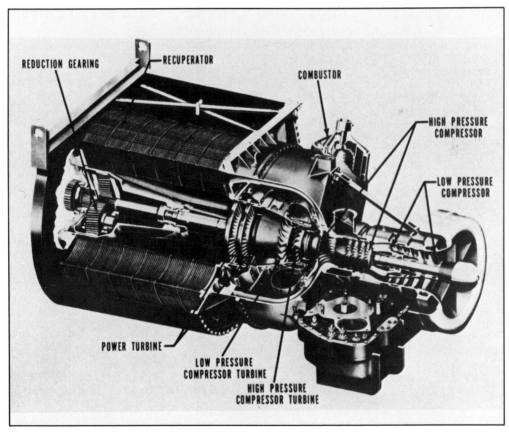

Cutaway drawing of the M1 tank engine. General Dynamics

Laser Weapons

The newest threat to American tanks like the Abrams are directed-energy weapons such as lasers.

One might assume that tactical laser weapon systems being developed both by the United States and others would be used to cut in half each other's tanks. However, the armor-piercing capability of current, and projected, future laser weapon systems are not as effective either in cost or in destruction power as the large number of antiarmor weapon systems already fielded in their respective inventories.

Lasers have already been fielded in target acquisition and communications systems by many armies around the world. Iraqi T-72 tanks had laser range finders. At present, though, no army has yet fielded laser devices specifically as weapons. But, even laser-emitting devices, such as a target designator or a range finder, can be employed as a weapon if it is aimed at a target it can damage.

Lasers produce an intense, focused beam of light that is more powerful than the brightest searchlight. Because of the human eye's great sensitivity to light, the unprotected and exposed tanker has a great deal to fear from current lasers and future laser weapon systems.

When struck by the intensified light of a laser, the optic nerve suffers a phenomenon known as photocoagulation in which the eyes can be damaged. If you are looking through a magnifying optic (sight, binoculars and so on) that doesn't have a laser filter, the optic's magnification will cause even more laser energy to travel into the viewer's eyes. The greater the magnification, the more serious the laser injury.

American tankers have already been issued ballistic laser protective spectacles (BLPS, for short). All variants of the Abrams tank are fitted with laser-filtered sights. Tankers are currently taught various techniques to minimize the effects of laser attacks, including maximum use of the Abrams thermal sights. Laser energy from range finders and designators will not pass through the outer lenses of the thermal sights.

American tankers are also told not to use direct view, magnifying optics—unless they have to. If they do, they use the lowest magnification possible. They also avoid staring at any one spot on the battlefield for too long and use scanning techniques instead. To reduce the laser hazard, tank crew members are also taught to use smoke to degrade laser capabilities and to suppress known or suspected enemy laser positions with direct or indirect fires.

Other directed-energy weapon systems being developed, both by American and Russian designers and engineers, are radio frequency weapons based on high-power microwave and millimeter wave sources and particle beam weapons, which seem to be the least developed because of their limited range capacity, and the large size imposed on such a weapon system due to the large amount of power needed to supply such a system.

The most likely directed-energy system slated next for US and Russian development would be radio frequency weapons. Unlike laser weapon systems which have one major technical weakness—the inability to operate effectively in rain, haze and heavy fog conditions—radio frequency weapons would operate not on an optical wavelength, as laser weapons do, but at radio frequencies. This makes them less affected by poor weather conditions.

A radio frequency weapon would produce a large amount of energy directed at enemy targets, thereby causing the entire electronic circuitry of vehicles or aircraft to overload and short-circuit themselves out of action. Electronic failures could also be caused in radar systems, radios and ammunition fuses by a radio frequency weapon that could be mounted on a wheeled or tracked vehicle.

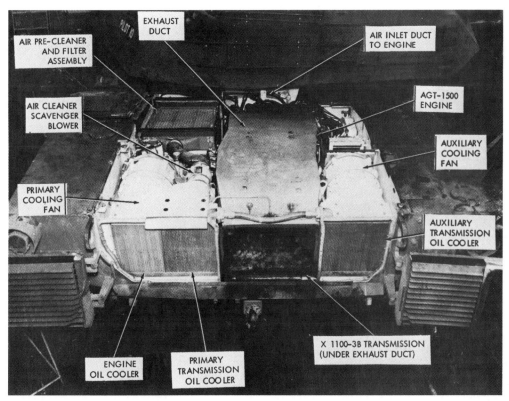

The AGT-1500 engine installed in an M1 tank.
General Dynamics

*Rear view of the cooling system for the
AGT-1500 engine.* General Dynamics

range of 280–300 miles. During the Gulf War, the US VII Corps vividly demonstrated that the M1A1's range was more than adequate to quickly reach its objective and accomplish its mission. The bottom line: In a trade-off between fuel economy and crew survivability, survivability should come first—that's the hard fact.

Crew Safety

Should the M1 tank be hit and penetrated, a number of innovative protective measures enable the crew to survive what would have been fatal explosions in the past. Ammunition and fuel stowage is compartmentalized, with forty-four main gun rounds being carried in the turret behind sliding armor doors.

Eight main gun rounds are stowed in a compartment in the hull and three on the turret floor, protected by spall-protection tubes.

In the event of a hit in the ammo bustle located in the rear of the turret, the blast of the resultant explosion is vented upward and out of the bustle through blow-off panels.

Halon Fire Extinguishing System

Adding to the survivability of the vehicle and its crew is an automatic fire suppressant system containing Halon 1301. The system includes seven dual-spectrum infrared detectors which sense the radiation characteristics of a

M1 tank turret at the factory, before being fitted to a hull. Michael Green

hydrocarbon fire, but will not give a false alarm because of stimuli from a flashlight, cigarettes, lighters or matches, sunlight, metallic insignia or red clothing. The sensors will detect a fire of eighteen inches in diameter at a distance of 1.6 yards within 1.5 to 6 milliseconds. The system will respond to a fire and will help suppress it in a few milliseconds before an explosion can take place. M1 crews still need to use hand-held extinguishers to completely put out fires.

Armor Protection

For protection against hits, the early-model M1 tanks had both standard welded-steel armor plate and special composite armor known as Chobham, which gave them significantly better protection, weight-for-weight, than any other existing armor in use in the early 1970s.

Since armor is the heaviest component on any tank, its placement is based on the probability of where it's most likely to be hit. As a result, special composite Chobham armor fitted to the M1 tank is on the sixty-degree frontal arc of the vehicle and other critical locations. The top, sides and rear of the vehicle are covered by welded-steel armor plate of varying thickness. The side skirts of the

M1 tank hull on the factory assembly line.
Michael Green

M1 tank are also made out of Chobham armor.

The Chobham armor fitted to the M1 tank, which gave it a revolutionary level of protection against shaped-charge weapons, was a late addition to the M1 tank design. Special armor was a requirement from the signing of the initial XM1 contract with the original contractors, Chrysler and General Motors. It was only by accident that the M1 tank program manager became aware of Chobham's development while the Army was formulating its requirements for the M1. Realizing its far-ranging advantages over conventional steel armor as then used on all American-built tanks, he quickly ordered that it be included in the M1 design requirement.

The major drawback to the Chobham armor is that it must be fitted in large, thick sections to be effective. As a result, the M1 tank took on a box-like appearance, a marked contrast to the rounded turrets of the M48 Patton tank or early-model M60 tanks, which were cast.

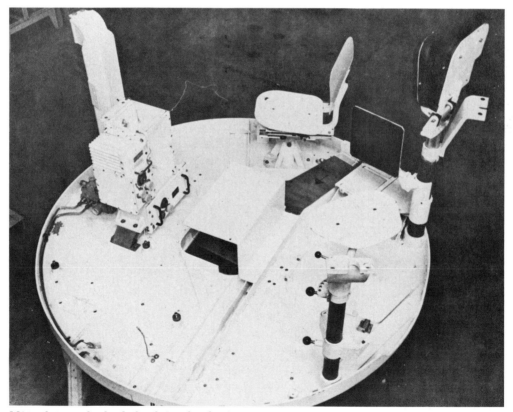

M1 tank turret basket before being fitted to its turret. General Dynamics

To demonstrate its survivability, early-model M1 tanks were subjected to live-fire tests in 1978 at Aberdeen Proving Ground, Maryland. An M1 tank was loaded with fuel and ammunition, fully instrumented with sensors and equipped with dummies similar to those used in automobile impact tests. Then, various types of ammunition that might be employed against US armor were fired at the idling M1 tank from representative engagement ranges. The M1 tank was not destroyed, and at the end of firing it was driven away under its own power.

Another test at Aberdeen Proving Ground added further proof of the M1 tank's survivability. An M1 tank was subjected to an antitank mine attack. The blast caused appreciable damage to some portions of the suspension system, but after short-tracking one side of the vehicle, the crew was able to start the tank and drive away from the test site. (Short-tracking means that the crew have shortened the length of the re-

The various components located in the M1 tank hull, below the turret basket. Michael Green

maining track around the remaining undamaged road wheels.)

One test was conducted on an M1 tank to see how it would survive a large overhead artillery air burst. This was simulated at Aberdeen Proving Ground by mounting an artillery warhead on top of a telephone pole and setting it off.

Overhead view of an M1 tank at speed. The M1 can reach speeds of 45 mph on level ground. General Dynamics

The M1 tank also passed this test with flying colors.

Chobham Armor

While much of the history and development of Chobham armor is still shrouded in secrecy, some generalized facts are known.

Chobham armor was discovered by a British scientist named Dr. Gilbert Harvey in 1965. Dr. Harvey worked at a secret military laboratory outside of London, England, near the village of Chobham from where the armor received its nickname. The official code name used by the British and American military was Burlington.

Using a variety of different materials ranging from metal alloys to ceramics arranged in a honeycomb fashion

M1 tanks waiting to attack during maneuvers. The US Army had to develop new tactics *to accommodate the advanced mobility of the M1 tank.* General Dynamics

encased in a steel armor box, Dr. Harvey discovered that shaped charge warheads from bazooka-like weapons, be they American, German or Soviet, couldn't penetrate the successive variety of material encased within this new type of armor. When a shaped charge warhead explodes, all the energy is channeled by an integral cone as a jet of extremely hot gasses that cut through conventional armor in the same way an acetylene torch cuts through steel. Chobham armor breaks up and dissipates the force of the gas stream.

This new development in armor protection was picked up by the people in charge of developing the XM1 tank. After being improved by American scientists, this new armor was fitted to both the Chrysler and General Motors test prototypes.

Reliability

Reliability is critical to mission accomplishment, and no other tank in the world has achieved reliability rates comparable to the Abrams. The M1 series' operational readiness rates exceed

This M1 tank in West Germany shows the closed-hatch position of the driver. The three periscopes mounted to the hatch provide an overlapping field of vision. Michael Green

Close-up of the 7.62mm M240 machine gun mounted on the loader hatch of the M1 tank. This machine gun is used to keep enemy infantry away from the vehicle. General Dynamics

ninety-five percent. That means that at any point in time, ninety-five out of every 100 tanks are available to perform their missions. Abrams tanks have been subjected to nearly 700,000 miles of grueling operational tests, ranging from winter tests in Sweden and Alaska to more than 200,000 miles in severe desert conditions. Egypt and Saudi Arabia selected Abrams tanks after conducting head-to-head competition between the M1 series and tanks from Brazil, France, Great Britain, Germany and the Soviet Union. These competitions took place in the harshest Middle Eastern desert conditions. The Abrams simply outperformed its competitors in that severe environment.

The M1 series further reinforced their reputation for rugged depend-

Overhead of loader's hatch on an M1 tank without the machine gun having been fitted. Most modern Soviet tanks have automatic loaders, doing away with the human loader found on American tanks like the M1. General Dynamics

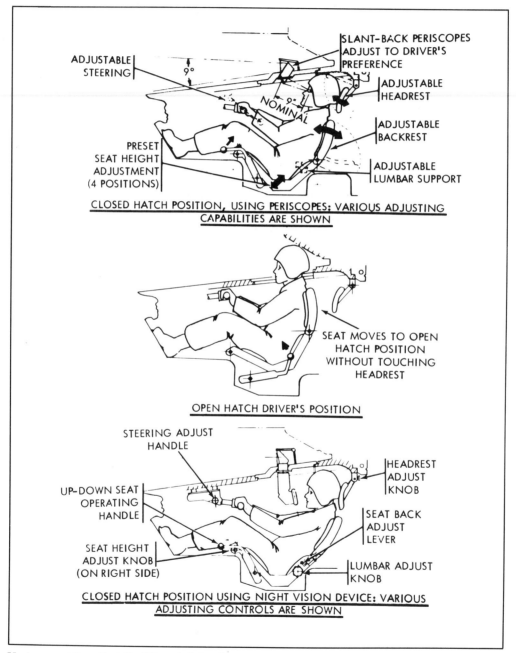

ADJUSTABLE
STEERING

SLANT-BACK PERISCOPES
ADJUST TO DRIVER'S
PREFERENCE

9°

NOMINAL 9°

ADJUSTABLE
HEADREST

ADJUSTABLE
BACKREST

PRESET
SEAT HEIGHT
ADJUSTMENT
(4 POSITIONS)

ADJUSTABLE
LUMBAR SUPPORT

CLOSED HATCH POSITION, USING PERISCOPES; VARIOUS ADJUSTING
CAPABILITIES ARE SHOWN

SEAT MOVES TO OPEN
HATCH POSITION
WITHOUT TOUCHING
HEADREST

OPEN HATCH DRIVER'S POSITION

STEERING ADJUST
HANDLE

HEADREST
ADJUST
KNOB

UP-DOWN SEAT
OPERATING
HANDLE

SEAT BACK
ADJUST
LEVER

SEAT HEIGHT
ADJUST KNOB
(ON RIGHT SIDE)

LUMBAR ADJUST
KNOB

CLOSED HATCH POSITION USING NIGHT VISION DEVICE: VARIOUS
ADJUSTING CONTROLS ARE SHOWN

Various positions that the M1 tank driver has when operating the vehicle. General Dynamics

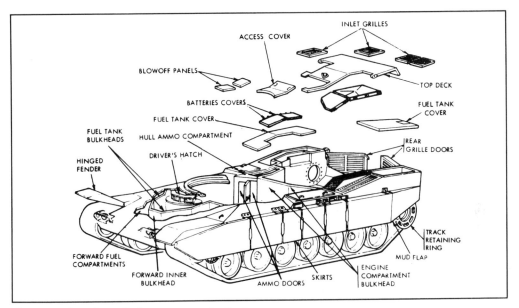

Cutaway drawing of the components that make up the hull and turret of the M1 tank. General Dynamics

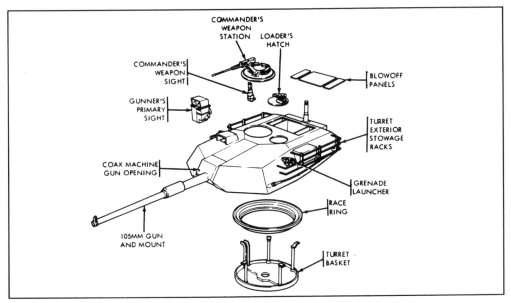

The major components of the M1 turret. General Dynamics

ability during its performance in Operation Desert Storm. In more than ten years of service with the US Army and now the US Marine Corps, the M1 series has logged over fourteen million miles on 7,000 vehicles. From the snows of the Arctic to the sands of the Sahara, the M1 series continues to perform in extreme climactic ranges from forty-five degrees below zero to 120 degrees above zero, Fahrenheit. Abrams tanks have proven repeatedly that they are rugged, reliable performers in any environment.

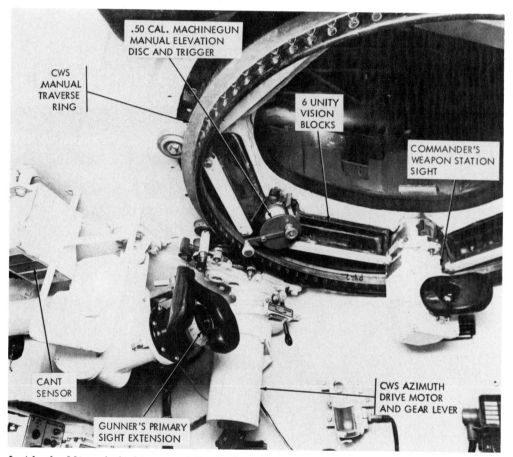

Inside the M1 tank, looking up at the tank commander's position. General Dynamics

The M1 tank has its own onboard smoke generator. General Dynamics

Tank Radar Warning Systems

Outside of making future armored vehicles less detectable targets, and keeping them out of sight as much as possible on tomorrow's battlefields, there will no doubt come a time when they must expose themselves to enemy observation and fire. Since passive armor protection will be limited to a certain extent on future armored vehicles, the US Army is looking to an integrated threat warning and reaction system being part of every vehicle protection system.

Much like the radar warning system mounted on current US Army attack helicopters that can tell a pilot that an enemy radar system is tracking his aircraft, or that an antiaircraft missile is on its way and from what direction, some future vehicles will feature an advanced computer-controlled warning system. This system will sense the trajectory of an incoming antitank shell or missile, and take action to prevent the vehicle from being hit. Chaff or a heavy smokescreen

might be produced to confuse and blind the enemy gunners, or smart munitions. Another type of protection may include active armor, which will involve sensors detecting incoming antitank rounds or missiles, and just before striking the vehicle a large cloud of very small steel ball bearings would be set off in front of incoming shells or missiles, hopefully destroying or deflecting the threat before the vehicle is hit.

In 1977 the Army tested an experimental automated combat vehicle system to detect and defend against guided antitank missiles. A model of the system built by Vought Corporation was installed in an M60A1 tank and successfully operated during a demonstration in which simulated missiles were fired at the tank.

The system used an omnidirectional optical sensing device mounted on the tank. When an antitank missile is launched, the sensing unit immediately picks up the infrared energy emitted by *continued on next page*

53

the missile. The energy is then converted into an electrical signal and fed into a computer inside the tank. The computer interprets this signal and simultaneously displays the information on a panel in front of the tank commander, and activates a warning system alerting the crew that the vehicle has been fired upon.

The computer will then activate one of two countermeasure devices mounted on the outside of the tank. One of these will act against antitank missiles that are being optically guided or flown along a laser beam to their target by producing a smokescreen from a smoke dispenser, hopefully in time to hide the tank from the gunner's view.

The second countermeasure device is a flare launcher for use against thermal-seeking missiles. If a thermal-seeking missile is fired at the tank, the flare launcher on top of the vehicle will shoot thermoflares, which produce higher levels of heat energy than a tank does to attract the missile away from the vehicle.

Although development is still at an early stage, the Army is constantly seeking to refine the basic concept. Other forms of sensors are being looked at, including using ultraviolet instead of infrared energy as a means of detecting antitank missiles in flight. Also being researched is the use of tank-mounted acoustic detection equipment to help detect and warn the tank crew of enemy helicopter gunships, or attack aircraft headed in their direction.

Much further down the line, the US Army may be looking for a very small laser weapon system that could be mounted on an individual vehicle. Again, the laser weapon system would be attached to an advanced threat warning system that would detect incoming enemy shells or missiles, and destroy them with a quick burst of laser light.

Chapter 3

Firepower

Two M1 tanks firing in the dark at the same moment. American M1 tankers know that four times out of five, the side that fires first in a tank battle will win. General Dynamics

Although the M68 105mm gun was used as the main armament on the first vehicles produced, the turret of the M1 was designed from the beginning to accept a 120mm gun at a later date.

The gun-turret drive and stabilization systems are hydraulically driven, electronically controlled and powered by an engine-driven pump. When the engine is off, a battery-driven auxiliary pump powers these systems.

Stabilization refers to very small onboard gyroscopes inside of tanks that sense any change in the aim of the main

M1 tank at the National Training Center, Fort Irwin, California, firing downrange. Greg Stewart

tank gun. They then readjust the gun to its original setting with appropriate corrections sent to the traverse and elevation motors attached to the main gun. This allows modern tanks to fire on the move while crossing uneven terrain. During World War II, all tanks had to come to a complete stop before firing so as not to move or spoil the aim of their guns.

Some American Army M4 Sherman and M26 Pershing tanks used during World War II were fitted with simple but crude gyroscopic stabilizers in elevation only. Unfortunately, the technology at the time was too unreliable for their successful use in action.

Full stabilization in both the azimuth and elevation of American tank guns didn't occur until the M60A1 tank was fielded in the early 1970s.

Stabilization of the main gun and turret on the M1 tank is achieved through rate gyroscopes, a hydraulic gun and turret drive, and an individually stabilized sight in the elevation mode. The gun is connected to the sight in the elevation axis with precision resolvers and the hydraulic system.

During World War II, most tank guns were aimed with nothing more than a telescopic or periscopic sight in which a series of graticules gave tank gunners and commanders a vague feeling for range and lead marks for shooting at moving enemy targets. Normally combat actions took place at under 800 meters with tank crews guessing how far away the enemy was and firing a couple of shots high and low until the range was obtained.

It wasn't until the 1950s that American tanks began being fitted with opti-

Looking forward over the turret of an M1A1 tank at the moment of firing. US Army

cal range finders mounted across the upper width of their tank turrets. While a big improvement over the earlier eyeball method of firing, longer range firing of tank guns was still very inaccurate.

In the 1980s, laser range finders as fitted to the M1 tank overcame all of the problems of optical range finders. A laser is aimed at an enemy target and a pulse of light is emitted which is then reflected from the enemy target and picked up by a receiving lens mounted on the M1 tank. A computer quickly takes the time for the laser light pulse to reach the target and measures the return time and com-

The 105mm gun can be seen here outside of the M1 tank turret. The 105mm gun was based on a British designed tank gun. General Dynamics

A 120mm gun before its installation in an M1A1 tank. General Dynamics

putes it into a range displayed as a digital readout for the M1 gunner.

The primary sight on the M1 tank presents the gunner with a constant display of range and an indication of the last range, and the letter F if there is failure in the fire control system.

The fire control system also includes a full-solution, solid-state digital ballistic computer; a thermal sight; a neodymium YAG laser range finder; and a gunner's auxiliary sight.

External elements of the primary sight system, protruding through the turret to the right of the gun, are protected by ballistic shield doors that are operated from inside.

Another feature of the fire control system, the muzzle reference sensor (MRS), allows the gunner to manually correct minor accuracy loss caused by gun-tube warp or bend by sending corrections to the ballistic computer.

Gun-tube warp or droop is the bending of the tank's main gun tube caused by uneven heating or cooling. The heat of the sun striking the upper surface of the gun tube will cause the gun to bend downward, resulting in tube droop. This is particularly a problem with long barreled guns like that found on the M1 tank. Excessive droop can cause tank rounds to completely miss their targets.

The digital computer, which is linked with the fire control system, accommodates changes in ammunition and ballistics data, and provides accurate lead correction for moving targets. Functioning of the fire control system is continually monitored by the computer. The computer also performs fire control system built-in test functions by direct interrogation to locate malfunctioning elements.

Data from wind and cant sensors and the range finder, plus lead angle information, are automatically fed into the computer. Other inputs, such as muzzle reference compensation, ballistic characteristics of ammunition being fired, tube wear, barometric pressure, ambient temperature and ammunition temperatures, must be set manually by the M1 gunner.

The current M1 fire control system also permits the gunner's primary sights to be used from the tank commander's station, giving him a complete day and night vision fire control capability. The commander and the gunner can both aim the main gun at the targets, and the commander's station is also equipped with a three-power-magnification sight for the .50 caliber machine gun, mounted on the top of the M1 tank turret.

M1 Tank Gunner

The gunner's primary sight (GPS), with its extension for the tank commander, is the main optical sighting instrument. It also includes the laser range finder, the thermal vision system and the gyro stabilized line of sight platform. The sight is protected by an armor steel cover with doors operable from within the turret. The gunner's auxiliary sight is an eight-power articulated telescope installed in the right side of the main gun mount below the coaxial machine gun.

The gunner has a computer that automatically receive the range from the laser range finder, and compensate for lead, crosswind and cant so that the gunner needs only to maintain the correct sight picture and fire. (Cant refers to when one side of the tank is higher than the other.)

The gunner's seat pedestal is mounted on the turret basket floor and is adjustable in both the vertical and horizontal directions. No adjustments are required when the gunner shifts from the primary sight to the auxiliary sight.

To operate the laser range finder the gunner needs only to lay on target and press a button to activate the laser. Normally, he would then fire. The range value or number is displayed in the

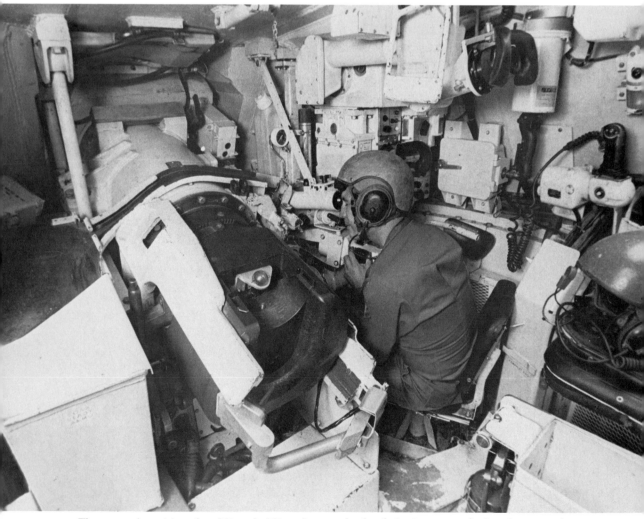

The gunner's position of an M1 tank. M1 tank gunners are taught to recognize enemy vehi- *cles by their signatures, be it noise or smoke.* US Army

gunner's and the commander's sight, so they can see if it appears correct compared to their estimate of the range.

The laser range finder can range on targets located 200 to 7,990 meters from the tank, with an accuracy of plus or minus ten meters.

If the range to the target is between 200 and 4,000 meters, the range is automatically placed in the ballistic computer. The range will appear in the range display of the GPS. If the target is between 4,010 and 7,990 meters, the range is not automatically placed in the ballistic computer. The actual range will appear in the range display of the GPS as flashing numbers. This feature is extremely useful in calling for fire since an exact range to the enemy will permit a precision location to be transmitted to the supporting artillery.

Thermal Sights

The thermal imaging system (TIS) provides the M1 fire control system with

The interior of the M1 tank, showing the gunner's controls. Michael Green

A 120mm gun mounted on a test stand, at the moment of firing. General Dynamics

night vision capability by presenting a thermal scene in the GPS eyepiece. The TIS picture can be viewed at three-power or ten-power magnification.

The TIS electronics unit (EU) generates the range and symbol data for the GPS. The EU and the power control unit (PCU) are on whenever turret power is

A 120mm armor-piercing fin stabilized discarding sabot (APFSDS) round used by the M1A1 tank. General Dynamics

on; that is, eyepiece symbols (range, ready to fire, malfunction) are generated whenever turret power is on. There are two different TIS reticles; the type depends on the date of production of the TIS. Earlier models have a rectangular box in the center of the reticle pattern, while later models have a square box.

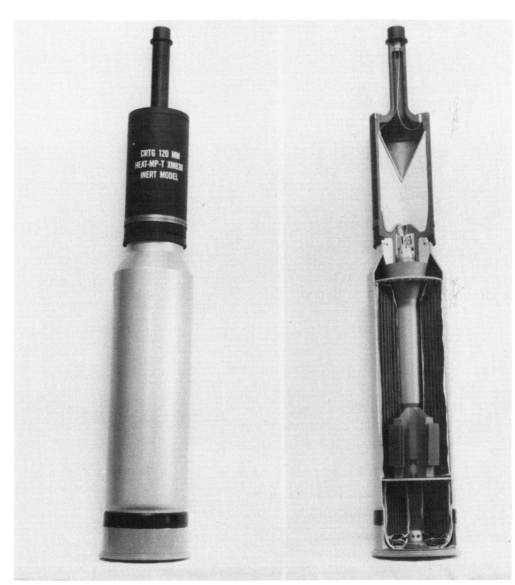

The second type of armor-defeating round that the M1A1 tank uses, known as a high- explosive antitank (HEAT) round. General Dynamics

Target scene information is detected by heat sensors in the TIS thermal receiver unit (TRU). This scene information is converted to electrical signals, processed by the EU, and sent to the image control unit (ICU) for display on a cathode ray tube (CRT). The CRT image is then optically projected into the GPS eyepiece for view by the gunner and commander.

The TIS uses range information from the laser range finder, which operates through the day channel sight. Therefore, both the day and night ballistic doors must be open during operation of the TIS. The shutter also turns off the day reticle illumination that can be seen when looking into the sight window from outside.

The TIS uses the same range information that the day channel does. Because of this, the TIS must be aligned or boresighted to the main gun point of aim every time the day reticle is boresighted,

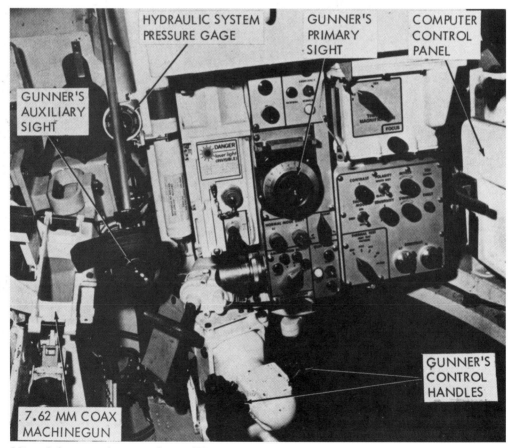

M1 tank fire control system. General Dynamics

normally once a day. It is critical to ensure that the daylight and TIS reticles are not aligned by superimposing one upon the other; the correct procedure is to refer each reticle to the same aim point on a distant target.

It is also important that the TIS picture is correctly adjusted. Target acquisition and identification can be seriously degraded with an incorrectly adjusted TIS picture. Misuse of some controls on the image control unit can cause the TIS picture to disappear.

The fire control system has also been used in a unique role, on occasion, to maneuver the vehicle when the driver's periscope becomes obscured or his night vision device fails, or there is not enough ambient light. In such cases, the gunner uses his TIS to lay the gun in the direction of travel and then tells the driver which way to turn to keep the gun centered over the front slope to maintain a heading, and whether to slow down or speed up to maintain interval during a road march.

COAX READY ROUND BOX
HOLDS 3300 7.62 MM
ROUNDS

BIN HOLDS
20 FIELD BOXES
OF 7.62 MM

LOADER'S
SEAT

Left front view of the inside of an M1 tank, showing both the 105mm gun and loader's seat. General Dynamics

M1 Tank Loader

The loader is at the left rear of the main gun and has a six-position adjustable swiveling seat. Loaders find their work is easier on the M1 than on other tanks even though their station is a bit cramped. They also have to learn a new maneuver when from a seated position they remove a round from the bustle rack and turn it to load. Most loaders can beat the five-second standard set for loading the main gun.

Forty-four rounds of 105mm ammunition are stowed in the turret bustle in racks behind sliding armor plate doors. Twenty-two of these rounds can be reached by the loader without leaving his seat. A knee switch operates the

The loader of an M1 tank places a live round into the breech of a 105mm gun. The M1 tank loader selects and loads ammunition an-nounced by the tank commander. He is also responsible for loading the coax machine gun. US Army

bustle compartment door covering these twenty-two ready rounds on the left side of the turret. The door also can be operated manually in an emergency. Blowout panels in the bustle roof vent any ammunition explosion to the outside. Three additional 105mm rounds are stowed on the turret basket floor to the left of the cannon in spall protection covers. Eight are stored in the hull behind the engine compartment bulkhead. This brings the total 105mm ammunition stowage to fifty-five rounds.

M1 Tank Commander

The commander's station permits observation in the seated position through both the extension from the gunner's primary sight and the sight for the .50 caliber machine gun. Six periscopes permit 360 degree vision. The three positions of the commander's platform allow him to observe standing with the hatch in the protected open position or at two heights with the hatch fully open. The commander's .50 caliber machine gun is electrically powered in azimuth, and is elevated manually.

The tank commander's main job is to command his vehicle. He controls the movement and fire of the tank through his actions and orders.

Stealth Tanks

In the past, vehicle survivability depended a great deal on the thickness of armor. As technology has improved, however, armored vehicles face attack from a number of weapon systems. Trying to protect one vehicle from all these weapons by adding more armor will become counterproductive due to weight and size of the added armor.

To get out of some of this dependence on conventional passive armor, which concentrates solely on defeating the terminal effect of antitank weapons, the US Army is looking for some nontraditional survivability features to prevent their destruction.

Making future armored vehicles as small a target as possible is one way of increasing survivability, but there are limits to this approach as long as a human crew will be carried aboard. A more logical choice when designing future vehicles is not to make the vehicle smaller, but to make it nondetectable to both ground surveillance radars and electro-optical systems—in other words, a stealth tank.

Producing a stealth combat vehicle is just now becoming possible due to advancements in composite material technology. There will soon exist the ability to produce an entire combat vehicle out of fiber-reinforced polymer (FRP) materials, including both the turret and hull. The rest of the vehicle components will be made out of other types of plastic laminates. The FRP hull and turret will have ballistic properties superior to steel or aluminum armor, plus offer a reduction in weight as compared to conventional types of armor found on many modern combat vehicles.

FRP has many desirable properties. One of the most advantageous properties of a combat vehicle fabricated out of FRP would be the ability to mold it with all-rounded surfaces. The turret or superstructures of such vehicles could be made in convex shapes, inclined at an angle to the horizontal. Such design traits would eliminate almost all of the radar traps found on present vehicles, thus reducing the vehicle's radar signature. The FRP of the vehicle would act as an antiradar-reflection material by absorbing radar waves.

Other advantages of a vehicle made out of composite material are many. For one, a composite vehicle would not corrode and would have a higher fatigue resistance. This would result in big savings to the military, with reduced maintenance and life-cycle cost.

Because composites are an excellent insulator, a composite hull and turret would help hide the tank from thermal-imaging devices. Since thermal-imaging devices depend on heat produced by people and vehicles to form a picture, any improvements in masking the heat produced by a future M1 tank would better hide the vehicle from observation, or heat-seeking warheads from antitank weapon systems.

Being a good insulator, a composite vehicle would also lessen the demands on the vehicle's heating and cooling systems. Most importantly, a composite vehicle would offer significant improvements in crew survivability because of the non-spalling nature of the material. In other words, if a composite vehicle were pierced by an antitank round, there would be no metal fragments to endanger the soldiers inside the vehicle.

And, finally, in this day of reduced budgets for weapon systems, composites would help to reduce production costs because there would be fewer pieces to assemble.

Chapter 4

M1A1

Provision for product improvements to the M1 tank were planned from the beginning of its development to help it keep pace on the modern battlefield with evolving Soviet military tank designs. As a result, five different models of the M1 tank have been produced, or are being produced.

The first prototype of the M1A1 tank. Fourteen M1A1 prototypes were built for test and evaluation by the Army. US Army

The original model, the (basic) M1, was produced from 1980 to January 1985; 2,374 M1 tanks were produced.

The second model, produced from 1984 to 1986, was the Improved Performance M1 (IPM1). A total of 894 IPM1 tanks were produced. The IPM1 was produced to take advantage of various improvements from the M1A1 program before the full-up M1A1 tank was ready for production. Some of these improvements include a beefed-up suspension with increased-capacity shock absorbers and reindexed torsion bars, various transmission improvements, improved armor protection, a modified final drive, the redesigned M1A1 gun mount, and the addition of the M1A1 turret bustle rack. The added weight (one ton) of the IPM1 tank has decreased performance only slightly.

The third model, the M1A1, or M1 with Block I Product Improvement,

started production in August 1985. In addition to the improvements fitted to the IPM1 tank, the M1A1's major characteristic is the German-designed M256 120mm smoothbore cannon. Along with the new gun are a number of associated changes to the fire control system, including a modified ballistic computer and gunner's control panel, modified reticles in the gunner's auxiliary sight (GAS) and reduced ammunition stowage.

In addition to the improved range and penetration performance, the 120mm gun has other advantages. Its fixed ammunition is slightly shorter than the 105mm rounds, and they use a partially combustible cartridge case. Only a small stub case remains after firing and it is ejected into a container. Thus, the problem of hot cartridge cases on the turret basket floor is eliminated. The larger diameter of the 120mm ammunition is, of course, a disadvantage

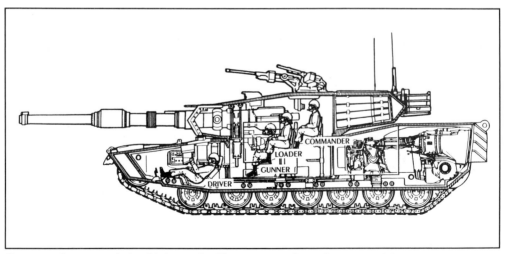

Cutaway drawing of the M1A1 tank. The main difference between the M1 and M1A1 *was the replacement of the 105mm gun with a 120mm gun.* General Dynamics

An early M1A1 prototype tank at Aberdeen Proving Ground, Maryland. The steel plates attached to the turret were designed to simu- *late the weight of a production vehicle.* US Army

Overhead view of an early M1A1 prototype tank. US Army

since it reduces the number of rounds that can be stowed. A total of forty 120mm rounds are carried, with thirty-four in the turret bustle and six in the hull. All of these are in separate compartments with blowoff panels.

The larger 120mm gun breech necessitated the redesign of the tank commander's and loader's seats. The tank commander's position has also been fitted with an arm guard in addition to the knee guard found in earlier model M1 tanks. The reconfigured turret incorporates redesigned turret blowoff panels, which are now in two pieces instead of three. The gun mantelet armor of the M1A1 tank also has been slightly modified to accommodate the larger 120mm gun tube. The M1A1 cross-wind sensor is fitted with a hooded top to better channel ambient wind.

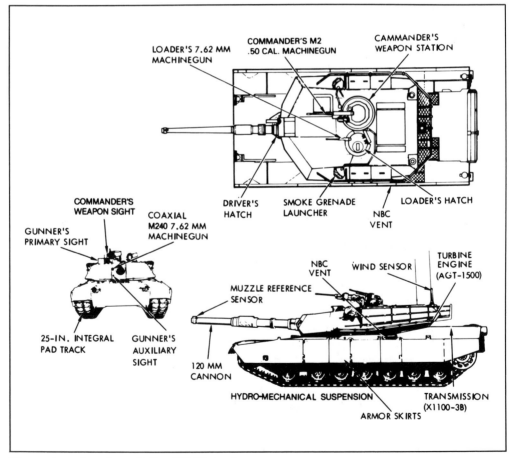

Three-view drawing of the M1A1 tank.
General Dynamics

Early-model M1A1 production tanks of the 3rd Infantry Division in West Germany, 1988.

US Army units in West Germany were the first to receive the M1A1 tanks. Michael Green

This M1A1 tank is training at Fort Hunter-Liggett, California, headquarters of the US

Army's Test and Experimentation Command. Michael Green

The Silver Bullet

The 120mm gun on the M1A1 tank fires various types of ammunition. The most important is the M829A1 APFSDST (kinetic energy round with long rod penetrator) dubbed the Silver Bullet by troops in the field. The M829A1 proved to be extremely successful against Soviet and Chinese made T-55, T-62 and T-72 tanks that had the misfortune to get in the way of it during Operation Desert Storm.

As one M1A1 tank commander put it, "If I saw it, I shot at it, hit it, killed it—routinely at ranges out to 3,500 meters [two miles]. One round was one kill and the secondary explosion left no doubt."

M1A1 tanks firing M829A1 rounds could be fired through sand berms five feet thick and destroy Iraqi tanks using them for cover and protection.

The M829A1 is one of a family of tank rounds fired from the M256

This rear view of an M1A1 tank shows the side and rear turret stowage racks. Michael Green

Even the M1A1 tank with its outstanding mobility can get stuck in soft ground. Michael Green

Night firing of the M1A1 in Alaska. It is a well-known fact that bullets fly slower when the air is very cold. This is due to colder propellent and denser air. The cold is also thought to have an effect on the gun-tube diameter. The instrument in the foreground is the projectile radar which is used to confirm exactly how much slower the round flies. From this data, a computer correction factor can be figured to ensure first-round hits at any temperature. US Army Cold Region Test Center

120mm smoothbore cannon mounted on the M1A1. Other combat rounds include the M829 (an early version of the M829A1) and the M830 High Explosive Anti-Tank (HEAT) round. There are also two training rounds: the M865 target practice round, the training counterpart of the M829 and M829A1, and the M831 target practice round, which is the training counterpart of the M830.

The M829 and M829A1 are the most lethal antiarmor rounds ever developed for an American tank.

Kinetic energy rounds such as the M829 and M829A1 are essentially large metal arrows made out of very dense material (depleted uranium). When fired from an M1A1 gun tube at high velocity, the energy they possess is enough to punch a silver dollar sized hole through the thickest of enemy tank armor. Penetration by any kinetic energy tank round normally causes very severe damage. Damage is caused not only by round penetration but also by the concussion of the hit, which shatters

Tanks with rubber pads are good for preventing road wear but can be extremely slippery on ice. Due to the extreme weight of each tank, a tank company can quickly pack the snow on any road into a gleaming sheet of ice. In an effort to remedy this problem, the program manager for Abrams tanks has developed ice cleats for the T-156 track. The ice cleats are bolted directly to the track on every sixth block. The Y shape of a cleat is visible directly below the fender on the near track. US Army Cold Region Test Center

both armor plate and interior turret and hull components of an enemy tank.

The energy given off when a kinetic round strikes an enemy tank is comparable to having two M1A1 tanks run head on into each other at high speed.

When the depleted uranium M829 or M829A1 round punches through an enemy's tank armor it breaks up into hundreds of very small particles. Traveling at very high speed inside the narrow confines of a tank's hull or turret, these small particles tend to bounce and ricochet off the vehicle's interior walls.

Within the first few fractions of a second after impact, the tank crew of a vehicle hit by a kinetic energy round are usually killed or severely wounded.

The M830 HEAT round carried onboard the M1A1 tank is designed to be used against lighter targets, such as armored personnel carriers, armored cars, trucks and so on. Instead of using a penetrator, the M830 has a high-explosive filler that is much more effective on lightly-armored targets.

The source of these redoubtable tank killers is the US Army Armament,

An M1A1 at Fort Greely, Alaska, with 12,000 foot Mount Moffit of the Alaska range in the background. The extremely demanding conditions at this Alaskan facility make it ideal for testing large weapon systems such as the Abrams. The severely cold, huge impact areas and miles of little used trails combine to test systems such as the Abrams to the limit. US Army Cold Region Test Center

Munitions and Chemical Command located at Rock Island, Illinois.

Secondary weapon system improvements to the M1A1 tank include a redesigned mount for the M240 coaxial machine gun, along with an improved ammunition feed tray. The M2HB .50 caliber machine gun mounted at the tank commander's position on the M1A1 tank is fitted with an electrical firing solenoid instead of the old manual trigger, which was difficult to use.

A larger rear turret bustle rack is fitted to the M1A1 tank, along with lengthened turret stowage boxes. Part of the reason for lengthening these boxes was to accommodate the equipment normally stowed in the left sponson box. This sponson-box area on the M1A1 houses the nuclear, biological and chemical (NBC) overpressure system.

This NBC system, the second of the main Block I improvements, supplies filtered, conditioned air to the M1A1 tank crew.

Soldiers prepare an M1A1 for an instrumented cold start in the world's largest cold chamber. US Army Cold Region Test Center

With the engine running, all hatches closed and a round in a closed breech, the system allows the M1A1 tank to operate in a contaminated environment without further protective gear. The system is set off automatically (along with an audible alarm in the vehicle's intercom system) in case of a sudden NBC attack, plus it also comes on automatically when the gunner selects the coax switch, taking the place of the old turret blowers. The individual crewmen of the M1A1 tank are also provided with micro cooling vests that circulate cool air over their bodies when operating in desert environments while wearing chemical protective clothing.

Other M1A1 improvements include a two-speed drive for the manual turret traversing mechanism, a locking device to hold the loader's hatch against the turret roof when fully open, a dual-fan

The M1A1 tank also featured a nuclear, biological and chemical (NBC) protection system—something the early-model M1 tanks did not feature. Faced with an Iraqi threat to use chemical weapons, the Army top brass decided to quickly field the M1A1 tanks from West Germany to Saudi Arabia. These M1A1 tanks are shown in a defensive position shortly before Operation Desert Storm began. US Army

Arctic tankers mounting a mine roller. Due to solidly frozen ground, mine rollers are the only way to go in the winter in Alaska. Note the VEMASID (vehicle magnetic signature duplicator) which is located behind the soldier on the tank in the partially attached configuration. The VEMASID is designed to project a magnetic signature out ahead of the vehicle, which is required since rollers are not effective against magnetically fused mines. Also on this tank is the T-158 (FMC Heavy) track which features removable pads as opposed to the T-156 track which has nonreplaceable pads. US Army Cold Region Test Center

An M1A1 tank with mine roller and VEMASID (not visible) and T-158 track ready to go. Notice that some rack pads have been removed. This is done in an effort to establish the best configuration for traction in snow. As might be expected, all track pads removed proved to be by far the best configuration. US Army Cold Region Test Center

personnel heater with an exterior air intake, and removal of the track retaining rings on the drive sprockets.

Some additional modifications considered Block II material changes were incorporated into M1A1 production tanks starting in late 1988.

One of the most interesting and highly classified modifications by the Army was the use of depleted uranium in the armor plate for the M1A1 tank. Although little information was provided by the Army for obvious reasons, it appears that machining techniques have been developed for the extremely dense material. This new armor greatly increases the penetration resistance of the M1A1 armor against kinetic energy rounds, something earlier composite armored M1 tanks were not as good at.

With this major improvement in armor protection, the M1A1 tank is called M1A1 HA (heavy armor).

Part of the Army's reason for announcing the new armor publicly was to present facts that would dispel myths about depleted uranium and allay potential public and worker fears. In fact, while not well known, depleted uranium has been used commercially for many years. For instance, commercial airlines use it for ballast on international flights, and the US Army has used it on the long rod penetrators for their kinetic energy rounds like the M829A1 for quite a while. Actually, there is so little exposure to radiation that a soldier would have to sit on top of the armor package for seventy-two consecutive hours to get the same

A prototype Abrams Recovery Vehicle (ARV). The ARV was not placed into service by the US Army. General Dynamics

exposure that television viewers get during seven average days of viewing.

The US Marine Corps had expressed a strong interest in fielding a fleet of 476 M1A1 tanks, but funding problems has led the Corps to consider buying only 221 (or fewer) M1A1 tanks in the future. Since the Marine Corps did not receive any of its M1A1 tanks from the factory until late 1990, the Corps borrowed 106 M1A1s from the US Army. These vehicles were enough to reequip two Marine Corps tank battalions for service in the Middle East. Transition training for the tanks and their crews was conducted at Twenty-nine Palms, a large Marine Corps base located in southern California.

Egyptian M1A1 Tanks

In 1988 Egypt and the United States signed an agreement allowing Egypt to co-produce up to 555 M1A1 tanks for their armed forces.

While the first twenty-five M1A1 tanks will be from American production lines, later tanks would come partly assembled so the Egyptians will build up

The first Abrams tanks sent to Saudi Arabia at the beginning of Operation Desert Shield belonged to the 24th Infantry Division (Mechanized) which is home-based at Fort Stewart, Georgia. US Army

experience in putting them together. In the longer term it is hoped that Egypt will be able to build many of the M1A1 tank components in-country.

More sensitive components of the M1A1 tank like the fire control system and armor would continue to be imported from the United States.

Operation Desert Storm

Abrams tanks, crewed by highly trained soldiers and marines, performed magnificently in Operation Desert Storm—routing the best Soviet tanks Iraqi troops had in the field. Of 1,956 M1A1s in the theater of operations, none were destroyed, four were disabled and four were damaged, but repairable. At least seven Abrams tank crews reported taking direct hits from Iraqi T-72 125mm main guns and suffered no serious damage. The Iraqi shells simply could not penetrate the Abrams tanks. At very close ranges,

The 24th Infantry Division (Mechanized) is the US Army's premier desert war fighting outfit, equipped with almost 200 105mm gun armed M1 tanks. Pictured are two M1 tanks of the 24th on patrol in Saudi Arabia during Operation Desert Shield. US Army

however, it is possible to penetrate the armor on an M1A1 tank.

American soldiers and marines using M1A1s dominated the battlefield. United States Marine reservists, in a single engagement, using Abrams tanks for the first time (thirteen tanks) and outnumbered nearly three to one, stopped thirty-four of thirty-five Iraqi tanks. In fact, during four engagements in four days, they stopped fifty-nine Iraqi tanks (thirty of them the top-line Soviet T-72) without losing a single American tank.

After 100 hours of offensive operations, the Abrams tanks had operational readiness rates above ninety percent. Especially noteworthy was a night move of more than 300 US Army tanks covering 200 kilometers (120 miles), without a single breakdown.

A 105mm gun armed tank of the 24th Division in Saudi Arabia. Deserts are not always barren sand dunes; Saudi Arabia has a mix of different types of desert terrain. This M1 tank of the 24th Division is shown in a mountain and basin desert combination. Mountains found in this type of desert are usually very rocky, jagged and cut by deep canyons. US Army

The Abrams tanks were faster, more mobile and able to outrange the Iraqi tanks. M1A1s had better guns, better ammunition, an exceptional thermal imaging system, better range finder, better fire control system and much better armor than the Iraqi tanks.

M1A1s did, in fact, dominate the battlefield.

While soldiers and marines were undoubtedly key to the human–machine interface that made success possible in the Persian Gulf War, Abrams tanks proved to be as effective as the US Army

The M1 Abrams tank of 2nd Lt. Christman A. Hampton, a platoon leader in Company C, 1st Battalion, 64th Armor, displays its agility as it bounds across desert sands in Saudi Arabia during a training exercise. US Army

and General Dynamics had predicted they would be.

One of the striking survivability lessons learned was the importance of having fuel and ammunition separated from the crew by armor, as it is in the M1A1. All the Soviet-designed Iraqi tanks had crew, ammunition and fuel located together in the vehicle. Time after time, Iraqi tanks suffered catastrophic losses because their tanks blew up when their armor was penetrated. The Abrams tanks suffered no such losses.

Mobility and speed also played a key part in the ability of coalition forces to complete the ground war in 100 hours. The daring dash across southern Iraq to the Euphrates River by US armor forces —covering some 200 miles in thirty-six hours and cutting off the Republican Guard escape to the north—effectively ended the war.

Three other M1A1 capabilities contributed to the success of American tank crews. The ability to fire accurately while on the move gave M1A1 crews an advantage over the Iraqi tanks, which had to

Early in the deployment of US Army tank units to Saudi Arabia, the Pentagon decided to substitute M1A1 tanks to units like the 24th Division which had been equipped with ear- *lier model M1 tanks. Here, an M1A1 tank is being repainted in desert sand tan colors in Saudi Arabia. US Army*

stop to fire their weapons. The ability to destroy targets from beyond 3,000 yards was another plus for the Abrams crews. The Iraqi tanks' effective range was under 2,000 yards, so American tanks could sit outside their range and fire on them. But, one of the most devastating advantages was provided by the thermal imaging sights (TIS) of the M1A1.

The TIS made it possible for American crews to see targets at night and through rain, sandstorms and smoke. The Iraqi tank crews did not have that capability. One Iraqi prisoner of war, who was a tank crew member, told a General Dynamics field service representative, " . . . it was not a fair war. We did not even know you were in the area when our tanks started blowing up."

The ability to see the enemy and engage him at extended ranges, while moving at high speed, with a deadly accurate fire control system and extremely lethal high-explosive antitank and kinetic energy rounds, made for a very one-sided ground war. In one case, an M1A1 kinetic energy round went through a sand berm surrounding an Iraqi tank, hit and went completely through the vehicle, then went through the berm on the opposite side of the vehicle.

From the standpoint of reliability, the M1A1 tank proved how wrong its critics had been. Moving a battalion of main battle tanks on a high-speed cross-country operation, while maintaining operational readiness rates above ninety percent, offered irrefutable proof of the inherent reliability of the gas-turbine-powered Abrams tanks. Critics who predicted the gas turbine engine would never last in the desert were proven wrong.

Two M1A1 tanks at the opening phase of the ground war. Operation Desert Storm showed that armor on the M1A1 tanks involved in combat actions against Iraqi tanks proved to be almost impervious to both T-55 and T-72 tanks's rounds. US Army

The Enemy

Prior to Operation Desert Storm, the Abrams main battle tank had never fired a shot in anger, or been tested in the heat of battle. American tankers looked with a great deal of expectation to see how their vehicles would perform against the Iraqi military's top-of-the-line Soviet-designed tanks.

While the Iraqi military had almost 6,000 various types of tanks in its inventory, most of them were older generation Soviet-built tanks or their Chinese-built counterparts. The pride-and-joy of the Iraqi military, and their most modern vehicle, was roughly 500 Soviet-designed T-72 tanks. There are fourteen identified variants of the T-72 tank in service with sixteen armies around the world. Besides the Soviet Union, there are also four other countries that produce their own T-72s.

Iraq had three different variants of the T-72 tank in service. Of the three variants, one is built in Iraq. Named the Lion of Babylon, this version and the other types of T-72 variants used by the Iraqi military tended to be concentrated mostly in the so-called elite Republican Guard units.

The various versions of the T-72 tank all mount a 125mm gun, a 7.62mm coaxial machine gun and a 12.7mm antiaircraft machine gun on the vehicle's turret.

Unlike the Abrams, however, which has a four-person crew, the T-72 tank houses only a three-person crew. The Soviet designers installed an electronically driven automatic loader in the T-72, which allowed the removal of the human loader. This also allowed the Soviets to build a smaller tank than the Abrams.

Unfortunately for T-72 users, the automatic loader has had its share of technical problems. Because the turret is so small and cramped, and Soviet safety measures are so primitive, occasionally a careless T-72 crew member has been grabbed by the autoloader and forcibly loaded in the breech of the 125mm gun, with the expected disastrous results.

The T-72 tank can carry thirty-nine rounds of ammunition, the M1A1 carries forty rounds. Soviet ammunition and fire control components such as vision devices and sights on the T-72 are grossly inferior to those found on the Abrams. This means that the T-72 could not fire its 125mm gun as fast, as far, or as accurately as could the Abrams.

M1A1 tanks employed during Operation Desert Storm consistently managed to see Iraqi tanks and engage them long before the Iraqi tankers could get within effective range to even see them or fire back at them. The T-72 does not have thermal sights like the Abrams. And when Iraqi tanks got the chance to even fire at the Abrams in combat, the inferior Soviet-built ammunition simply bounced off the advanced armor of the M1A1 tank.

Powered by a 780 horsepower diesel engine that is transversely mounted in the engine compartment, the T-72 can travel on a dirt road at an average speed of 35 mph. On a paved road it can get up to almost 40 mph. The T-72 has a range of almost 300 miles.

The fuel tanks on the T-72 extend along the right side of the hull top. In combat action during Operation Desert Storm, American tankers found that a single round in this area usually caused a catastrophic explosion, resulting in the entire T-72 turret being blown off the hull of the vehicle.

While the various T-72 variants used by the Iraqi military all had thick, well-sloped conventional cast steel armor and more advanced composite armor fitted, it didn't seem to matter much against the 120mm gun in the M1A1 tank. Any Iraqi T-72 tank hit by a 120mm round would disappear in a ball of flames.

The average T-72 tank weighs in at about forty-one tons. In contrast, the M1A1 weighs almost seventy tons.

While the Abrams quickly proved its superiority over Iraqi T-72 tanks, in the last few years the Soviet Union has fielded improved versions of both the T-72 and newer tanks. Fielded only in front-line service with the Soviet Army, the T-80 has been demonstrated to both the Syrian and Indian armies. Like the Abrams, the T-80 has also been fitted with a gas turbine engine, although new models have been built with diesel engines.

The T-80 has the same 125mm gun as found on the T-72 tank. Besides firing standard tank rounds, some T-80 tanks can also fire through their 125mm guns, the AT-8 Songster antitank missile. The AT-8 Songster missile is used to engage targets at long ranges like the Abrams, tow missile teams or even American helicopters like the Apache gunship.

The missile itself is radio-controlled by the T-80 gunner who guides the missile to its target. The missile guidance box is mounted on the right side of the turret roof of the T-80, in front of the vehicle commander's cupola and can be removed, if required, and stowed.

Very similar in overall layout to the T-72 tank, the T-80 has an automatic loader and three-person crew. Armor protection has been beefed-up, with improved types of multilayered composite armor on the front of the hull. The 125mm gun tube is fitted with a thermal sleeve and flume extractor like the T-72 and Abrams tank. Mounted on the front of the turret are banks of electronically operated smoke discharges.

The T-80 is still not fitted with thermal sights like the Abrams, but must depend on much less advanced night vision devices.

Chapter 5

M1A2

As part of preplanned product improvements collectively known as Block II (The M1A1 tank was Block I), new modifications resulted in the M1A2 being developed. The modifications included an improved nonrotating com-

The newest member of the M1 family is the M1A2 tank. Shown is a prototype M1A2 tank.
General Dynamics

mander's weapon station (ICWS), a commander's independent thermal viewer (CITV), an intervehicular information system (IVIS) or battle management system and provisions for installing a driver's thermal viewer.

Prior to the availability of the CITV, holes were cut in the turret roof forward of the loader's hatch on late-production M1A1s to permit the later installation of the new thermal viewer.

If fitted to the M1A2, the driver's thermal viewer will allow him to see under the same visibility conditions as the gunner and the tank commander when they are using the gunner's primary sight. Thus, he could drive without assistance from them in smoke or fog. Although originally intended for the first production of the improved M1A1, both the commander's independent thermal viewer and the driver's thermal viewer were postponed until later production because of cost restrictions. The driver thermal viewer (DTV) has been fully tested and type classified. If at some time the Army decides to procure the DTV, it may be installed in all M1 series tanks without modification to the vehicle. The DTV is designed to fit directly into the mounting points used for existing driver passive viewer. Also deferred to a later date is an identification, friend or foe (IFF) device. This is intended to identify friendly tanks on the battlefield and to prevent their accidental destruction by friendly fire.

In the past, the Army focused heavily on armor and other passive defensive measures as basic tank improvements. In the M1A2, they sought to optimize an already proven design but also to recognize that the best defense is a good offense. Thus, improvements incorporated in the M1A2 are designed to make the tank more lethal and easier to use in battle.

New munitions combined with new sighting equipment, the Abrams now has the ability to take on helicopters and other low-speed flyers. The improved laser range finder and improved vehicle electronics combine to provide better and faster ballistic solutions and hence improved probability of hitting an enemy tank.

The ability to mass combat firepower at the right place and time is crucial to fighting the AirLand battle. Each member of the combined arms team becomes a critical piece of that fight. The key is the ability of the commander to orchestrate each piece to maximize the potential for success by overwhelming the threat with shock, firepower and massed force. The M1A2 provides the commander with this ability through its superior command and control system, integrated intervehicular displays at the driver's, gunner's and tank commander's positions, and vehicle electronics driven by state-of-the-art microprocessing software. Through the onboard position/navigation system (POS/NAV), the tank commander now has the ability to navigate his tank by preplotting his course on a tactical display (CID) and transferring this data to the driver who then merely steers to the course indicated on his driver's integrated display (DID). The tank commander is then freed up to communicate on the radio and to transfer information digitally to other tanks through his intervehicular information system (IVIS). This is crucial to supporting the commander's fight and to provide instantaneous and real-time information transfer on unit locations and individual tank positions as well as threat data while maintaining secure communications.

Once the battle is joined, the commander's independent thermal viewer (neither the M1 nor M1A1 tank had this feature) allows the tank to acquire more targets faster than the M1A1. This hand-off capability is designed to allow the tank commander to independently search for targets, acquire, automatically slew and lock the gun to the target

(hand-off to the gunner), then search again for the next target while the gunner is engaging the first target. The CITV can scan by area automatically for silent watch operations, or manually from the tank commander's position. The improved commander's weapon station with eight vision blocks significantly increases all-around visibility during closed-hatch operations. The M1A2 incorporates all of the survivability features of the M1A1 and then goes a step beyond by providing dual redundant digital and power busses that wire the electronics systems together

Side view of a prototype M1A2 tank. One of the most important improvements to the A2 version is the commander's independent ther- *mal viewer (CITV), which is located on the right side of the turret, in front of the loader's hatch.* General Dynamics

and provide back-up for each other while providing information and power routing. For example, the hull and turret electronics units are identical parts and in case one is damaged, the other provides back-up for mission critical functions.

While the US Army has ordered sixty-two M1A2 tanks, the production line prove out will be accomplished mostly through the sale of 465 tanks to Saudi Arabia which also has an option for the purchase of an additional 235 tanks. This will mark the first time in history that the United States has sold to a foreign government, more sophisticated equipment than it has in its own inventory.

In May 1991, the US Congress began considering money for the Army to

The CITV enables the commander to view the entire battlefield, separate from the gunner, while still directing the main gun firing. General Dynamics

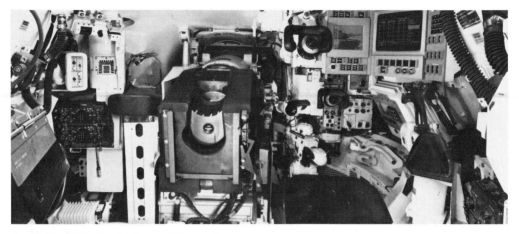

Inside the M1A2 tank. General Dynamics

cover a program to upgrade existing M1 and IPM1 tanks to M1A2 status. Currently, there are 2,374 M1s and 894 IPM1s. This modernization program, if approved, will help preserve the United States' industrial base so that we do not lose the ability to build tanks. This means that General Dynamics will continue to build Abrams tanks until the next generation tank is fielded sometime after the year 2000.

The proposed upgrade or conversion program envisions a minimum sustaining rate of 240 tanks per year, enough to maintain one tank plant open for eight to ten years or until Block III begins production.

Testing the M1A2 Tank

M1A2 prototype tanks have already been subjected to a wide variety of rigorous tests conducted by the US Army.

At White Sands Missile Range, New Mexico, in 1991, prototype M1A2 tanks were blasted with simulated nuclear

devices and exposed to gamma and neutrodose radiation that would be given off by tactical nuclear weapons in combat. At Aberdeen Proving Grounds, Maryland, Army evaluators fired numerous antitank rounds at M1A2 prototypes to test the strength of its armor protection systems. Technical teams at Aberdeen Proving Grounds also dissected an M1A2 prototype tank piece by piece to run tests on its mechanical, electrical and electronic systems.

In central California at Fort Hunter-Liggett, five M1A2 prototype tanks crewed by soldiers from the Fort Hood, Texas-based Test and Experimentation Command's Combat Experimentation Battalion engaged in force on force simulated combat against an opposing force from the 4th Infantry Division at Fort Carson, Colorado, in 1991.

The tank crews from Fort Hood, Texas, had spent two months transitioning from their M60A3 tanks to the M1A1, which was followed by forty-two days of intensive M1A2 training. They were also subjected to intensive platoon-level gunnery before going up against the opposing force which was going to be using standard M1A1 tanks.

The purpose of this simulated combat activity was to stress the M1A2 and its crews under conditions it would face in combat. The actual results of the tests performed on the prototype M1A2 tanks is classified information, but will provide the US Army with the information needed to determine how much better the M1A2 tank is than the M1A1 tank.

Abrams Replacement

Still in the very early concept stage, the US Army is already working on a replacement vehicle for the Abrams tank. Due to the extreme time lag in fielding a new tank (up to ten years or more), the Army did not want to waste any time in designing a new tank for the twenty-first century.

The new main battle tank will be the centerpiece of the Army's armor force of the future. That tank, currently undergoing concept development, is the Block III.

Two major defense contractors are already working on the project. The first is a partnership of General Dynamics (builders of the M1 Abrams) and FMC Corporation (builders of the M2 and M3 Bradley Fighting Vehicle). The other is Teledyne Continental Motors.

The developers are building the Block III from the ground up. The Block III will incorporate the best of new and emerging technologies, plus the lessons learned from Operation Desert Storm. Some of the priorities established by the US Army for this new tank include lethality, survivability, strategic deployment capability and sustainability.

The Block III program is the product of two separate and distinct programs. The first is the Block II, which evolved into the current M1A2 tank. The Block III program was originally going to be an even more improved version of the Abrams tank that would have eventually been called the M1A3 tank.

But, at the same time the Army got funding for the two block improvement programs, the Armor Family of Vehicles Task Force completed its study. It called for a system designated as the Future Armored Combat System, or FACS. Eventually the FACS and the Block III concept came together as part of Armored Systems Modernization Program (ASM, for short). As a result, the Block III program is no longer seen as an Abrams modification, but as a completely new tank.

ASM's focus is to design a common chassis that will not only accommodate Block III requirements, but also meet the requirements of the Engineer's Combat Mobility Vehicle, the Advanced Field Artillery Systems, the Future Infantry Fighting Vehicle, the Line-of-Sight Anti-tank System and the Future Armor Resupply Vehicle for ammunition.

The advantages of having common chassis are numerous. Having a maintenance mission that requires serving only one system simplifies logistic requirements.

With the collapse of the Soviet Union and its former military might being divided between a number of newly-created republics, Soviet Army tank development has come to almost a complete halt.

The future funding of a Block III tank may be called into question by the US Congress. Much like the B2 Stealth Bomber, a Block III tank was designed to counter a Soviet military threat that no longer exists. Congress may assume that the current fleet of M1A1 tanks may be adequate in dealing with any third world conflict.

Index